Quantum Computing and Code

Principles for the Next Great Leap

Table of Contents

Chapter 1. Introduction

Navigating the ever-evolving landscape of technology can be an expedition like no other. Our Special Report on "Quantum Computing and Code: Principles for the Next Great Leap" takes you on a fascinating journey into the next frontier of computing. While this topic might seem intricate and highly technical, our approachable and sensible narration ensures a stroll through quantum fields feels as familiar as your morning coffee. You're invited to step into the world of qubits and quantum calculations, unveiled in a way that is comprehensible even without a PhD in Physics. This report is your roadmap to understanding this transformative technology and its potential impact on the world around us. Discover, learn, and join the quantum leap with us.

Chapter 2. Unveiling the Quantum Realm

To truly appreciate the revolution of quantum computing, we need to first familiarize ourselves with the world of quantum mechanics. This is a field of science that, at its core, is about the smallest particles in our universe – the micro realm where our usual, so-called 'classical' laws of physics cease to operate as expected. Instead, particles in the quantum realm follow a different, extraordinary set of rules.

2.1. Quantum Mechanics - A New Perspective

The birth of quantum mechanics was initiated in the early 20th century, a time when classical Newtonian physics was challenged by some of the curious phenomena observed at the atomic and subatomic level. A whole new set of principles was called for, revealing itself in the form of quantum mechanics.

The most fascinating principle perhaps is 'superposition', which postulates that particles can exist in multiple states at once, only resolved to a definite state when observed. Take a coin for instance. In our classical world, a coin spun mid-air is either in a heads or tails state, but in the quantum realm, it can be both heads and tails simultaneously till it's observed.

Another important principle, 'entanglement', defies our classical understanding of information transfer. When two particles are entangled, a change in one instantaneously affects the other, irrespective of the distance between them. This non-local effect perplexed even Albert Einstein, who famously dubbed it "Spooky action at a distance".

2.2. The Cube of Two States - Qubits

Embracing these rich quantum principles, we turn towards Quantum Computing. The fundamental building block of a quantum computer isn't a bit but what's known as a 'qubit'. The qubit is all about the superposition principle. In the classical world, a bit represents a zero or a one. But a qubit, harnessing superposition, can represent a zero, a one, or both at the same time.

Until someone checks a qubit's value, it is spinning both up and down simultaneously, as if the coin were constantly spinning in mid-air. When you check it, similar to observing the coin, it does fall into one state or the other.

Importantly, as more qubits are entangled, more computational power is leveraged. If you double the qubits, you double the computational capacity exponentially. This potential scalability is part of what makes quantum computing incredibly powerful.

2.3. Quantum Circuits and Computation

A quantum computer processes information using quantum circuits, which leverage the principles of superposition and entanglement. In essence, you can perform many calculations at the same time, which enables a quantum computer to solve certain types of problems exponentially faster than classical computers. A quantum computer's ability to speed up calculations using uniquely quantum effects is known as 'quantum speedup'.

Quantum speedup holds the potential to bring about major breakthroughs in fields such as cryptography, where quantum computing's inherent strengths could lead to deciphering currently uncrackable codes, and in material science, where quantum simulations could lead to new discoveries.

A key challenge in harnessing this power, however, lies in maintaining 'quantum coherence' — the quantum state of qubits — long enough to perform operations, a state easily disrupted by environmental factors like temperature and electromagnetic radiation.

2.4. Quantum Error Correction

Given their peculiar nature, qubits are vulnerable to errors due to environmental interferences. To tackle this, an area of research called quantum error correction has thrown up promising techniques to detect and correct potential errors, so as to maintain the integrity of the quantum information.

For instance, a technique called 'surface code' uses a 2D array of qubits, some for storing information and others for checking and correcting errors. Critics argue that the surface code currently requires an impracticably large number of qubits, but advances in qubit technology is expected to make it feasible.

2.5. The Quantum Leap: Implications and Promise

As quantum computers become increasingly viable, it's clear we're on the cusp of a new computing paradigm. Knowing how to harness and navigate these technologies will have profound implications for various fields, from material science to cryptography, from artificial intelligence to healthcare precision.

For society, the quantum leap has begun, and it will continue to evolve with our understanding of the quantum realm. As these advancements ensue, whether one's particular realm of interest is science, technology, or simply the future of humanity, contemporary familiarity with quantum computing will increasingly become a central tenet. This exciting journey into the quantum realm, the next frontier in computational advancement, is just beginning. And with this, you've now taken your first step into the world of quantum computing - welcome aboard!

Chapter 3. Basics of Quantum Computing: A Gentle Introduction

Quantum computing is a rapidly advancing field that combines principles from both computing and quantum mechanics. By utilizing the unusual properties of quantum physics, quantum computers aim to solve problems far more rapidly and efficiently than classical computers. But what are these properties, and how do they work? Let's explore.

3.1. Quantum States and Superposition

Quantum mechanics is known for its counter-intuitive principles, and one of the easiest to begin with is that of superposition. When we think of a conventional (or "classical") bit in computing, we know that it can be in one of two states, 1 or 0. However, a quantum bit, or "qubit", can exist in a state that is both 1 and 0 simultaneously. This is known as superposition.

The state of a qubit is more accurately represented by a probability. When measured, a qubit in superposition has a certain probability of being 0 and a certain probability of being 1. Only when a measurement is made does the qubit "collapse" from its superposition into one of the definite states.

3.2. Quantum Entanglement

Another key property of quantum mechanics is entanglement. Entanglement allows pairs or groups of qubits to become linked such that the state of one qubit is directly connected to the state of the others—no matter how far apart they might be. This means when we know the state of one qubit in an entangled pair, we immediately know the state of the other.

This link remains, even if the qubits exist on opposite sides of the universe. This property has profound implications for information transfer and potentially for complex calculations, making it an integral aspect of quantum computing.

3.3. Quantum Gates and Operations

Classical computing uses logic gates to perform operations on bits. Similarly, quantum computing also uses gates – but these are referred to as "quantum gates".

A quantum gate is a mathematical function that manages the state change for a qubit. Importantly, these gates can operate on a qubit in superposition, altering probabilities and changing not only individual states but also entanglement between qubits. Some of the most commonly used quantum gates are the Hadamard Gate, the Pauli-X Gate, and the CNOT Gate.

It's worth noting that quantum gates differ significantly from classical gates in that their operations can be undone. When a conventional logic gate takes input, it generates output, and there's no way to recover the original input. But a quantum gate can take a qubit as input, transform it, and then be reversed to give the original state back. This property is a consequence of quantum gates being unitary—each gate has a corresponding "undo" operation.

3.4. Qubits and Quantum Circuits

A quantum circuit is a sequence of gates and transformations performed on multiple qubits to achieve a specific output. The order and types of gates used can drastically impact the output. Designing quantum circuits is therefore a challenging and crucial part of quantum computing, and many optimization algorithms exist to find the most efficient configuration to achieve a given output.

Quantum computers can manipulate many qubits at once due to the property of superposition. This enables the potential for massive parallel computations, where multiple computational paths are explored simultaneously, consequently boosting performance for specific tasks.

3.5. Quantum Computing vs Classical Computing

Understanding the fundamental differences between quantum computing and classical computing is key. Classical computing, based on the binary digit or bit, is excellent at performing many tasks. However, they fail to efficiently solve certain problems—like factoring large numbers, optimizing complex systems, and modeling quantum physics.

Quantum computing, utilizing the qubit, superpositions, and entanglement, can handle these complex tasks with ease. It promises to revolutionize fields from cryptography to drug discovery, bringing about a new era of technology.

Bear in mind that current quantum computers are still in experimental stages. Challenges with coherence times, error correction, and physical implementation mean that while the potential of quantum computers is jaw-dropping, we are still in the early stages of turning theoretical potential into reality.

In essence, quantum computing is a dramatic departure from classical computing, pushing the boundaries of what we understand about computers and information. By harnessing the fundamental principles of quantum mechanics, it lays the foundation for an entirely new way of approaching complex problems giving us new tools to shape the future of technology.

3.6. Conclusion

Quantum computing is a subject of immense potential and complexity. While understanding its underlying principles can be challenging, it nonetheless offers a fascinating insight into how the future of computing might look.

By figuring out how to harness the peculiarities of the quantum world into a new model of computation, we might unlock solutions to problems that currently seem impossible. It's a leap into the challenging but exciting depths of the quantum realm, and every step forward we take has the potential to revolutionize countless areas of life.

Chapter 4. Digging Deeper: Qubits and Superposition

Symbolizing the classic bit in the universe of quantum computing, a qubit, or quantum bit, is the fundamental unit of quantum information. While a conventional bit can represent a 0 or 1, a qubit can represent a 0, 1, or any superposition of these two qubit states. Now, if you're scratching your head at the term 'superposition,' don't worry—you're not alone. It's this profound quantum concept that we'll be exploring in great depth in this segment.

4.1. Unmasking Qubits

A qubit is visually depicted as the state of a vector residing in a two-dimensional space. The vector's two base states—often labelled $|0\rangle$ and $|1\rangle$—embody the fundamental qubit states, akin to the 0 and 1 states of a standard bit. However, the magic of qubits lies in their ability to exist in a blend or 'superposition' of these states.

Mathematically, a qubit $|\psi\rangle$ in superposition, can be expressed as:

$$|\psi\rangle = \alpha|0\rangle + \beta|1\rangle,$$

where $|\alpha|^2 + |\beta|^2 = 1$, and α and β are the probability amplitudes. The sum of the squares of the absolute values of these amplitudes tells us the probability of finding the qubit in state $|0\rangle$ or $|1\rangle$ when measured. The state of the qubit immediately post-measurement collapses to the measured state. This binary outcome introduces an element of probability intrinsic to quantum algorithms.

4.2. The Essence of Superposition

Moving on to the peculiar nature of superposition—the key to quantum system's power—it's frequently misunderstood to mean that a qubit is in both $|0\rangle$ and $|1\rangle$ states simultaneously. However, a more suitable description would be that the qubit exists in a state that, upon measurement, could result either in a $|0\rangle$ or $|1\rangle$, depending on the determining probability amplitudes.

Projecting to the traditional notions of computing, you can think of superposition in terms of machine instructions. Instead of executing either instruction 0 or instruction 1, quantum computing exploits superposition to examine both directions simultaneously, leading to exceedingly improved computational capabilities.

4.3. Measuring Qubits

Crucial to understanding the behavior of qubits and their superposition is the act of quantum measurement. On measuring a qubit, the superposition collapses to either a $|0\rangle$ or $|1\rangle$. After this, the qubit cannot return to its original superposed state. The results of quantum measurement are probabilistic, which means you can only determine the probability of the outcome, not the precise result, before the measurement.

To illustrate, consider a qubit in a superposition state of $|0\rangle$ and $|1\rangle$, with equal probability for either outcome. Measuring this qubit 100 times, we anticipate approximately 50 measurements each of $|0\rangle$ and $|1\rangle$, but the exact number might not be 50-50 due to its probabilistic nature.

Naturally, this attribute of unpredictability throws a wrench into classical computing ideas and is a matter quantum computing has to contend with. The various techniques to mitigate, harness, and even exploit this unpredictability form the basis of many quantum algorithms.

4.4. Quantum Entanglement

One of the most intriguing and counter-intuitive quantum mysteries is that of entanglement. As Einstein called it, "spooky action at a distance", two or more qubits could be intertwined in such a way that the state of one is instantly correlated with the state of another, regardless of the intervening distance. This crucially impacts a system with multiple qubits, adding an extra layer of depth to the mind-bending quantum computational prowess.

The entanglement property, combined with superposition, triggers an exponential growth of the computational space with every added qubit. For instance, while two classical bits can exist in one of four possible states, two qubits can exist in any superposition of these four states, thereby creating a larger compute space.

4.5. The Bloch Sphere Representation

To help visualize qubits and their states, we use the Bloch Sphere. This sphere represents $|0\rangle$ and $|1\rangle$ at its north and south poles, respectively, while superposition states are points within the sphere. The bloch vector's length is always 1, echoing the principle of conservation of probability. Each point inside or on the surface of the sphere shows a possible state in which a qubit can exist.

```
[.Bloch Sphere]
image::bloch-sphere.png[Bloch Sphere]
```

The sphere's 3D model perfectly accounts for the two cornerstones of quantum mechanics: superposition and entanglement. It helps grasp the fact that a qubit's state involves all possible mixtures of $|0\rangle$ and $|1\rangle$, and it encompasses a two-dimensional complex Hilbert space, a linear vector space with structures that allow geometric interpretation.

4.6. Gate Operations on Qubits

Like classical computing, quantum computing uses gates. However, quantum gates act on qubits through rotation on the Bloch Sphere, thereby manipulating their probability amplitudes. A quantum gate changes a qubit's state from its initial position to a new point on the sphere according to the specifics of the quantum gate operation.

Noteworthy among these gates are Pauli-x, Pauli-y, and Pauli-z gates, known as bit-flip and phase-flip gates, which alter the destination positions of qubits on the Bloch Sphere. Hadamard (H) gate, which puts qubits into superposition, is another pivotal gate in quantum computation.

4.7. Transition from Classical

In essence, diving into the realms of qubits and superposition requires a paradigm shift. Classical computing principles, though beneficial in paving the path to understanding, at times can encumber tackling quantum concepts. Qubits extend beyond simple 0s and 1s. They traverse a space of uncertainty, being uncertain till measured, and even then carrying only a probabilistic certainty.

Scope for just slightly more proficiency exists in binary operations before progressing further—using the quantum equivalent of 'bits' is like driving in fourth gear when you've only learned up to third. It's not impossible to manage, but it calls for a little bit of 'pushing the boundaries'.

In our journey through quantum computing and code, we've now skimmed the surface of qubits and superposition. As the core elements of the incredible power and potential of quantum computing, their intrigue and complexity are the gateways to galvanizing computational breakthroughs. The ability to operate on multiple states simultaneously and to impact profound quantum entanglement differentiates quantum computing from classical and paves the way to solutions previously thought beyond reach.

As we delve deeper, growing comfortable with these quantum idiosyncrasies, we'll continue expounding on the effects these phenomena have on computational speed, scope, and capabilities. A glimpse into quantum algorithms exploring these exotic capabilities awaits in the subsequent chapters.

Chapter 5. Quantum Gates and Circuits: The Building Blocks

Quantum Gates and Circuits are the vital components of any quantum computing system. In classical computing, the basic resources data is binary; it's either a 0 or a 1. However, in the realm of quantum computation, data exists in a state that encompasses a spectrum of possibilities, a state of both 0 and 1 simultaneously - a trait that is leveraged by quantum gates and circuits.

5.1. The Basics of Quantum Gates

Just as classical computing relies on specific operations, or gates, quantum computing also has its own set of quantum gates. They have strange sounding names like Hadamard, Pauli-X, Pauli-Y, Pauli-Z, and CNOT to name a few. These aren't just made up names, however, each gate signifies a certain transformation that can be applied to a qubit.

The Hadamard gate, for example, takes a qubit that's in one of the base states $|0\rangle$ or $|1\rangle$ and changes it into a state of superposition, where it can be either $|0\rangle$ or $|1\rangle$ with equal probability. Meanwhile, Pauli-X, often referred to as the bit-flip gate, swaps the state $|0\rangle$ with $|1\rangle$, and vice versa.

These transformations are carried out through linear operations applied to the state of the qubits. To better understand this, you might visualize qubits as vectors, and a quantum gate as a rotation or a reflection of this vector in a multidimensional space, known as Hilbert space.

5.2. Two-Qubit Gates and Entanglement

So far, we have discussed gates that interact with single qubits, but there are also multi-qubit gates. A key type of two-qubit gate is the Controlled NOT (CNOT) gate. The extraordinary capability of this gate is that it allows us to create quantum entanglement — a phenomenon where two qubits become intrinsically linked, and the state of one qubit is immediately connected to the state of another, no matter the distance between them.

The CNOT gate performs the operation of flipping the target qubit if the control qubit is in state $|1\rangle$. Therefore, if we apply a Hadamard gate on the control qubit, placing it into superposition, and then apply a CNOT gate, we create a Bell state, an example of a maximally entangled state. If a measurement is now made, the result will be either $|00\rangle$ or $|11\rangle$ - indicating the entanglement of the qubits.

5.3. Building Quantum Circuits

Joining these quantum gates together forms a quantum circuit. However, the computation doesn't run gate-by-gate. Quantum mechanics operates by the principle of superposition and wave function, allowing the entire circuit to be addressed all at once, unlike classical circuits.

This is where quantum computing gains its exponential computational speed and power, but it also presents a design and debugging challenge due to this 'all-at-once' operation. Understanding how to design and build efficient quantum circuits from the ground up is an ongoing field of study lest we end up with noisy and error-prone outputs.

5.4. Gate-Based Quantum Computing

The most common and studied model of quantum computation is gate-based quantum computing. Just as classical bits are manipulated with logical operations in classical computers, a gate-based quantum computer uses a sequence of quantum gates to manipulate qubits.

Using a universal gate set, any operation can be performed by a sequence of quantum gates from this set. In theory, just using the earlier mentioned Hadamard, CNOT and Phase gates (another commonly used quantum gate), any algorithm can be performed on a quantum computer.

Developing more efficient gate sequences to perform desired transformations is a large part of the research in quantum algorithms. The discovery of new gate sets and optimizing their usage can lead to faster, more accurate quantum computations.

5.5. Quantum Gates in Quantum Error Correction

Despite the promise of powerful computational ability, quantum computation is highly sensitive to environmental noise, making quantum error correction (QEC) an integral part of quantum computing.

QEC uses specific quantum codes and the fundamental principle of quantum gates to handle and correct errors. This includes gate errors, which can occur due to imperfect calibration or decay during the gate operation time. Recent advancements are helping the research field to steadily reduce these errors, bringing us closer to the goal of robust, practical quantum computers.

In conclusion, quantum gates and circuits form the core fabric of the world of quantum computation. How we manipulate these gates and how we construct circuits will largely determine the efficiency of quantum computers. As we continue our study in this field, we'll see groundbreaking advancements and paradigms that will revolutionize computation in ways we can hardly imagine today. The quantum leap awaits.

Chapter 6. The Quantum Advantage: Speed, Power, and the Future

Understanding the entity of quantum advantage begins with acknowledging the capabilities of classical computers. Current computing technology disassembles computation tasks into binary processes, the most foundational units of information or 'bits.' These binary digits, 0 and 1s, are adeptly manipulated by the computers to perform complex calculations and execute functions with astonishing speed.

Your smartphone, laptop, or even the server farms that power the internet, all deploy this binary system. However, the 0s and 1s have their constraints, particularly when dealing with particular complex problems encompassing vast data sets and intricate calculations. An ideal example of such a situation includes the simulation of quantum systems, like molecular interactions, where each additional particle exponentially whips up the complexity of the calculations.

6.1. A Quantum Leap in Computing Power

That's where quantum computing comes into play. Contrary to classical bits, quantum bits or 'qubits' embrace the oddities of quantum mechanics to handle intricate problems more effectively. A single qubit can denote a 0, a 1, or both 0 and 1 concurrently owing to a phenomenon called quantum superposition.

Furthermore, qubits can be entangled using quantum physics principles, enabling them to act as a cooperative unit. Changing the state of one qubit in an entangled pair instantaneously impacts the other, no matter how far apart they are. This unique property facilitates swift and efficient information processing surpassing anything classic computers can manage.

Quantum computing takes advantage of these properties to conquer problems that would take conventional computers hundreds, even thousands of years, to solve within seconds or minutes. The computational power quantum computing delivers could enable monumental changes in various sectors such as cryptography, drug discovery, financial modeling, and artificial intelligence.

6.2. The Quantum Speed Advantage

The superposition and entanglement of qubits give quantum computers the potential to perform calculations exponentially faster than classical ones. In some cases, quantum algorithms can deliver faster and more accurate results with fewer computational steps. This inherent superiority has been termed 'quantum speedup.'

Quantum speedup could significantly affect fields reliant on complex computations. In cryptography, for instance, quantum computers could crack codes and ciphers much quicker than classical counterparts. Similarly, when modeling molecular interactions for drug discovery, quantum computers could examine numerous molecular structures simultaneously, accelerating the search for promising compounds.

6.3. Deeper Dives into Quantum Power

Quantum computing does not just promise quicker computations. The power of a quantum computer extends beyond mere speed improvements. Quantum computers' potential to simulate complex quantum systems is a feat impossible for classical computers sans severe approximation.

In areas like materials science and chemistry, simulating complex quantum systems could lead to the discovery of new materials or drugs. Only quantum computers can replicate the dynamism and subtlety of such systems, creating unprecedented opportunities for scientific breakthroughs.

6.4. Quantum Future: A Glimpse into What Lies Ahead

The quantum computing field, though in its infancy, presents immense opportunities. Its transformative potential is visible in several theoretical and practical applications, promising to redefine our approach to problem-solving.

However, it also introduces new challenges. For instance, reliably operating quantum computers at a large scale necessitates maintaining quantum states known as 'quantum coherence.' It's an intricate process requiring extremely low temperatures and exceptional isolation from the outside environment. Solving these issues calls for persistent cooperation between scientists, engineers, and industry experts.

The quantum future also urges us to reconsider aspects of data security, given quantum computers can theoretically break encryption algorithms. The field of post-quantum cryptography already explores this concern, aiming to create algorithms resistant to both quantum and classical attacks, preserving our privacy and safeguarding our digital infrastructure.

In conclusion, the quantum advantage is more than just a speed or power boost. It represents a fundamental shift in how we approach computation, with the potential to revolutionize fields from finance to pharmaceuticals. While substantial challenges lay ahead in the journey to realize large-scale, fault-tolerant quantum computers, the promise they hold instigates ongoing research and investment, paving the way to a truly quantum leap in computation.

Chapter 7. Challenges in Quantum Computing: Addressing the Conundrum

Quantum computing, while potentially groundbreaking, faces various challenges. The pursuit to leverage this technology's unique properties is like a high-stakes race, with the finish line obscured with numerous obstacles. Erroneous sentiments might paint these as deterrents; quite the contrary, these challenges serve as keystones for the progression of quantum computing.

7.1. Physical Constraints and Quantum Errors

In the quantum realm, aspects like qubit stability and quantum error correction present significant obstacles. Quantum coherence, the unique property of qubits to exist in multiple states, is incredibly fragile. Any external interaction can disrupt this state—a phenomenon known as "decoherence."

Maintaining a coherent state for a practical duration is a feat requiring an exotic workaround. Techniques like using traps or supercooling environments have made strides in this area, but these solutions introduce new hurdles. For instance, supercooling requires very low temperatures (-273 degrees Celsius) hard to maintain, and quantum traps often fail to fully isolate the qubits from their noisy external environment.

On the flip side, quantum errors—something traditional computing doesn't grapple with—pose another challenge. As these errors are not just errors of the qubits, but errors of the quantum state itself, traditional error correction codes cannot mend them. Efforts are underway to develop quantum error correction algorithms that can manage these uniquely quantum blunders, but this field remains in its infancy.

7.2. Scalability and Infrastructure

Scaling quantum computers while maintaining fault tolerance is an immense challenge. Ensuring a large number of qubits can maintain consistent and reliable interactions is a hurdle that researchers are striving to eliminate. These challenges get exponentially complex with an increase in the number of qubits.

In contrast to classical computing wherein doubling the transistors doubles the power, quantum computing follows a different approach—one where doubling the quantum bits squares the computational power. This obliges robust quantum architecture, which is currently underdeveloped.

Infrastructure brings another set of challenges—multi-qubit gates, quantum interconnects, cryogenic engineering, measurement amplifiers, and error correction hardware—all pivotal to the success of a quantum computer, are still nascent technologies.

7.3. Software and Algorithms

Quantum programming bears little resemblance to classical programming. New programming languages need to be developed to utilize quantum hardware optimally, which demands massive education and adaptation on behalf of coders and programmers.

Finding problems suited for quantum computing poses another obstacle. While certain problems like integer factorization and database searches have been identified, more extensive research is needed to identify which problems quantum computers can solve better than classical computers and develop algorithms for them.

7.4. Security and Ethics

The arrival of quantum computers will indeed shake up our current cryptographic systems and potentially break most of the encryption techniques used today. The cryptanalysis power of quantum computers is a legitimate concern, and the transition to quantum-resistant cryptographic algorithms is inevitable.

Likewise, ethical issues need to be addressed before quantum computers become mainstream. The potential for misuse is enormous - from hacking into guarded systems to weaponization of quantum capabilities. Regulations must predate these potential threats, ensuring a protective layer against misuse.

7.5. Conclusion: Embracing the Challenges

We are yet unsure when a practical, scalable quantum computer will be produced. These challenges might sound daunting, but they are merely architectural issues to be mitigated by further advancements and stepped-up research.

The conundrum of quantum computing isn't so much about overcoming the challenges, but steering the way the technology evolves based on how we address these issues. As in any field, the avenues that seem laden with difficulties often hold the most reward.

Through consistent research and collaboration, we can create a new era for computational power. The journey is long, the hurdles real, but the destination—unparalleled computing—undeniably worth it. Keep in mind the familiar adage, Rome was not built in a day; likewise, the quantum realm will need time to fully materialize in our tangible world.

Chapter 8. Powerful Applications: Cryptography, Optimization and Beyond

Right from the genesis of computer science, professionals and enthusiasts alike have been on the quest to solve increasingly multifaceted problems. Quantum computing, a New Age marvel, appears poised to meet these challenges head-on, pushing the boundaries of what conventional computers are capable of. It is thus only fitting that we examine some of these applications, starting with two of the most salient questions facing the digital world today: cryptography and optimization.

8.1. Quantum Cryptography: The Secure Future

Drawing from the fundamental mechanisms of quantum mechanics, quantum cryptography offers unanticipated new directions for secure communication. Primarily, it leverages the concept of superposition and entanglement to accomplish this.

Superposition, the ability of a quantum system to exist in multiple states simultaneously, empowers quantum cryptography with an alternate way of encoding data. In this new encoding scheme, any act of observing or measuring the quantum system - say, an eavesdropping attempt - disturbs its state, alerting the communicating parties immediately.

Complementing this, entanglement - a uniquely quantum connection shared between particles regardless of the distance between them - brings about correlated units of information. This aspect can be used to generate a shared secret key between two parties, a key that is incredibly hard to intercept. Irrespective of the distance between the parties, any tampering becomes evident instantaneously.

8.2. Shor's Algorithm: Cracking Classical Encryption

Not all applications of quantum computing in cryptography safeguard security. Named after mathematician Peter Shor, Shor's Algorithm stands as a glaring example of how quantum computing can potentially dismantle existing cryptographic systems.

The algorithm depends on the number factorization problem, the basis of many encryption methods today, including RSA. The RSA algorithm works on the premise that factoring large numbers is computationally expensive for classical computers. Shor's Algorithm, however, can factorize such numbers in polynomial time, thereby seemingly placing all RSA-encrypted messages at risk.

The implications of Shor's Algorithm are enormous for our current information security infrastructure - but it's important to note that we are still a long way from practically implementing this algorithm on a quantum computer. In the interim, this challenge has sparked interest in developing post-quantum cryptography that would remain secure even in the face of powerful quantum computation.

8.3. Quantum Key Distribution

Quantum Key Distribution (QKD) serves as a practical application of quantum cryptography, further strengthening security. QKD uses quantum mechanics to guarantee secure communication, providing a method to generate and distribute encryption keys between two parties without the risk of interception.

Per the principles of QKD, if an eavesdropper attempts to intercept the quantum information, the intrusion will alter the state of the system. This change will be detectable by the communicating parties, enabling them to take preventive action.

BB84, a protocol developed by Bennett and Brassard, is an early example of QKD. It encompasses the aspects of superposition and quantum entanglement, highlighting the real-world prospects for quantum secure communications.

8.4. Quantum Computing for Optimization

Optimization problems are prevalent in various sectors, from logistics to machine learning, finance, and beyond. Classical algorithms tackle optimization problems, but they often struggle with problems of significant complexity. Quantum computing, through its inherent parallelism and ability to explore a large solution space, could provide more efficient solutions to these intricate issues.

Quantum Annealing, a quantum algorithm designed to find optimal solutions, exemplifies this capability. Designed to find the lowest energy configuration (the minimum) of a system, it can be extended to real-world optimization problems which involve finding the most efficient, least-costly or most profitable solution.

8.5. Beyond Cryptography and Optimization

The power of quantum computing, while highly prominent in cryptography and optimization, extends beyond these fields. Quantum algorithms such as Quantum Fourier Transform and Quantum Phase Estimation have profound implications for a multitude of disciplines such as chemistry, materials science, and drug discovery.

The application of quantum computing in these areas is still in nascent stages and, no doubt, we will uncover more breakthroughs and the realization of theory into practice as technology progresses.

It's safe to say that we are indeed on the cusp of the next great leap in computing, with quantum technologies poised to redefine how we tackle the world's most complex problems. The journey, however daunting, promises to be exciting and profoundly transformative.

Chapter 9. Quantum Code: Bringing Quantum Principles to Programming

The defining aspect of quantum computing is the shift from classical bits used in conventional computing to quantum bits or qubits. Unlike classical bits that remain in a specific state at any given time (either 0 or 1), qubits, thanks to the principles of quantum mechanics, can be in a superposition of states, existing in both 0 and 1 states simultaneously. This capability, coupled with a phenomenon known as quantum entanglement, is why quantum computers promise exponential speed-up over classical methods for certain types of computations.

9.1. Understanding Qubits

Qubits, even more so than the silicon transistor, are the fundamental building blocks of quantum computing. They are the quantum equivalent of classical binary bits but come with superpowers that classical bits lack, namely superposition and entanglement.

In a classical computer, a bit's value is either a 0 or a 1. However, a qubit can be 0, 1, or a superposition of both. Superposition is a quantum mechanical idea where a quantum state can be in multiple states at once. When we measure a superposed state, it collapses into one of its constituents states, but until that measurement, the system is in a blend of states, giving quantum computers their massive parallelism.

Entanglement, another quantum phenomenon exclusive to qubits, describes the deep connections between two particles. When qubits are entangled, the state of one qubit cannot be described independently of the state of others. They form a single unified system and changes to one will instantaneously affect the other, no matter how far apart they are. This profound correlation leads to incredibly synchronized computing capabilities.

9.2. How Quantum Computing Translates to Programming

Quantum programming entails writing codes that direct the operations of a quantum computer. These operations, also known as gates, manipulate qubits to compute your results. Unlike classical programming, where operations are binary (true or false), quantum operations take advantage of superposition and entanglement, allowing for a broader and more versatile range of actions.

Quantum programming languages such as Q#, developed by Microsoft, or Quantum Assembly (QASM), make use of this new paradigm to write quantum computing algorithms and operations. These languages have unique operations called quantum gates which are used to manipulate the quantum state of a system. These gates work primarily in two ways: alter the probability distributions of the various states of a qubit, for instance, causing a 0 state to become a 1; or entangle two qubits together so their states become intertwined.

It is also worth noting that quantum computing is not meant to replace classical computing, but rather to complement it. Quantum algorithms often interleave classical and quantum operations - a technique known as "hybrid quantum-classical computing."

9.3. Quantum Programming in Practice

A code in a quantum program typically does three things. It first initializes a quantum system in a certain state. This particular setup provides an equal-chance for the qubits to be in either 0 or 1 state.

Next, quantum operations take action in the form of quantum gates that manipulate the quantum states, weaving them through superposition and entanglement. The final step is measurement which forces each entangled qubit to commit to a binary state.

As with many things in quantum computing, writing a quantum program is conceptually distinct from conventional programming. It is less about determining the variables' step-by-step flow and more about devising a series of transformations that take the system from its initial state to a final state that provides a solution. This fundamental rethinking of programming methods may provide a unique foundation for advancements in machine learning, cryptography, and many other technologies.

9.4. Potential Limitations and Challenges

Despite the promising potential, quantum programming and computation also come with challenges. For one, since qubits must be kept in a quantum state in order to function, they are susceptible to interference from environmental conditions, a problem known as "decoherence." The problem of error correction is also more complex in quantum computers.

Furthermore, due to the requisite of quantum physics, quantum computing is an incredibly complex field, and quantum programming requires a steep learning curve. A fundamental grasp of linear algebra and complex numbers is needed and an understanding of the principles of quantum mechanics can be beneficial.

9.5. The Quantum Future

Quantum computing is still in its early days, but the potential applications are staggering. From breaking secure cryptographic codes to accelerating the discovery of new drugs, the potential areas for the application of quantum computing are nearly endless.

For programmers interested in joining this quantum leap, a solid grounding in classical computing principles will also be essential for successful quantum programming. The most proficient quantum programmers will be those who are not just adept at manipulating qubits but can also immerse themselves in the multidimensional world that quantum computing represents.

The world of quantum computing is vast and complex, but with the necessary investment in learning and understanding, programmers everywhere can stride confidently into this new era of computation. Despite the challenges that lie ahead, the future of quantum code and computation is undeniably promising and exciting.

Chapter 10. Current State of Quantum Computing: Technology and Market Insights

Quantum computing is at an emergent stage and it's ready to come into its own with progressive developments across a swath of industries and scientific pursuits. The current status of quantum computing offers an extensive vista of accomplishments and challenges. Concurrently, the market's readiness and response to this cataclysmic technology are key elements in the assessment of quantum computing's present state.

10.1. Quantum Computing Technology: Current Developments

The first two decades of the 21st-century witnessed astounding progress in quantum computing technology. Companies such as IBM, Google, and Microsoft along with startups like Rigetti Computing and D-Wave have made significant strides in the race to build a functional quantum computer.

IBM made a splash in 2016 when it put the first quantum computer in the cloud, the IBM Quantum Experience, offering the public the ability to experiment with a 5-qubit quantum computer. This was a huge step forward in the evolution of quantum technology and served as a harbinger for the growth of quantum computing services.

Google's quantum supremacy announcement in 2019 set a milestone in quantum computing. They developed a processor named Sycamore that could perform a calculation in 200 seconds, which the fastest supercomputer at the time would require almost 10,000 years to complete.

Microsoft's Quantum Development Kit focuses on building a software ecosystem relying on "topological qubits." These are more robust to environmental noise, allowing for error correction and improved functionality.

The Canadian firm D-Wave offers quantum annealers specifically designed for optimization problems. Quantum annealing represents a niche within the quantum computing domain that could have substantial potential applications across industries.

These endeavors mark the beginning of an exciting new chapter in the world of computing, with a rapidly growing body of hardware and software underscoring the readiness of the technology.

10.2. The Challenges in Quantum Computing

Parallel to these developments, quantum computing also faces significant hurdles that prevent its complete mainstream adoption. Building a fully functional quantum computer—capable of executing complex computations reliably, is a feat yet to be achieved.

The issue of 'decoherence,' where qubits lose their quantum state due to environmental noise, poses a major challenge. Despite advances in error correction mechanisms to counter this, creating an environment where qubits maintain coherence over a significant duration is an ongoing roadblock.

Another challenge is the scaling issue. While small-scale quantum computers are becoming increasingly commonplace, the quest for a large-scale, error-corrected quantum computer continues. The difficulty arises from the need to couple multiple physical qubits to form a single, logical qubit that can operate with high fidelity.

10.3. Market Insights: Quantum Computing

The current market valuation of quantum computing is promising. According to MarketsandMarkets, the global quantum computing market is expected to grow from $472 million in 2021 to $1.765 billion by 2026, at a Compound Annual Growth Rate (CAGR) of 30.2%. This growth is predominantly driven by the increasing demand for quantum computing in drug discovery, cryptography, and optimizing complex systems, among other sectors.

In terms of industry, the banking and finance sector looks to be at the forefront of adopting quantum computing, along with healthcare and defense. These sectors have vast amounts of data that could benefit immensely from the forecasting abilities of quantum algorithms.

Presently, North America dominates the quantum computing terrain, due to the concentration of majority of the market's leading players and the heavy investments in research and development. However, other regions such as Europe and the Asia-Pacific are also significantly investing in quantum computing research and applications.

10.4. The Quantum Race: Nation-State Involvement

The strategic importance of quantum computing hasn't escaped governments worldwide. The US, China, Canada, the EU, and Australia, among others, have initiated multi-billion-dollar national quantum initiatives.

These quantum ventures serve dual purposes - to foster technical advancements in quantum computing and to build a skilled workforce for the increasing quantum economy. This form of strategic involvement suggests the transformative potential of quantum computing and its pivotal role in future geopolitical scenarios.

In conclusion, the current state of quantum computing depicts an exciting mixture of groundbreaking technological achievements and substantial challenges. Alongside, market insights indicate potential growth and a keen interest from different sectors in integrating quantum computing into their operations. The next phase of this technology's evolution will undoubtedly be extraordinary, with profound implications for several industries and scientific domains.

Chapter 11. Is Quantum Computing the Future: Insights, Predictions and Perspectives

Quantum computing, a sector once viewed as a distant dream of the future, is rapidly becoming a reality. With the development of new and advanced technologies, we are witnessing a quantum leap, that is, a transition from classical computers to quantum ones—machines that base their operation on the principles of quantum physics.

11.1. The Basics: Defining Quantum Computing

To better understand quantum computing, it is essential first to define some critical terms and principles. A quantum computer operates using qubits (quantum bits) rather than the bit we're familiar with in classical computing. While bits in a classical computer can take on one of two states, 0 or 1, a qubit—through superposition—can exist in multiple states simultaneously. In essence, it can be in a state of 0, 1, or both 0 and 1 simultaneously.

This capability allows quantum computers to process a larger set of data than their classical counterparts. Moreover, the principle of entanglement in quantum mechanics allows qubits, once entangled, to share an instant connection regardless of their physical distance, enabling faster calculations and a substantial increase in processing power.

11.2. Technology Intersection: Quantum Computing and Artificial Intelligence

Quantum computing, bolstered by the principles of quantum physics, intersects with the growing realm of Artificial Intelligence (AI). The massive computational power of quantum computers opens prospects for AI, given AI's voracious appetite for processing power and fast computations. Machine learning algorithms, a subset of AI, stand to be revolutionized as quantum computers could significantly expedite learning processes and data analysis.

As an example, think about optimization problems. In these cases, quantum annealing—a quantum analog of simulated annealing—could offer an edge. Quantum annealing leverages superposition and entanglement to find the minimum (optimum) of a function. This process could drastically reduce AI's time to identify patterns in data or optimize complex logistical problems.

Normalization issues surrounding quantum models of AI are being resolved progressively, which implies a bright future for the interaction between these two cutting-edge technologies.

11.3. The Quantum Advantage: Observations and Potential Applications

Given the quantum advantage— the ability for quantum computers to solve problems which classical computers find computationally demanding—it's predictable that the quantum computing landscape will have wide-ranging implications across multiple industries.

In pharmaceutics and healthcare, quantum computing could help develop new medicines by modeling molecular interactions at an unprecedented rate. In finance, the improved computational capabilities of quantum computers could potentially revolutionize risk modeling and data analysis, enabling real-time and potentially more accurate predictions. Environmental scientists could benefit from quantum computing by creating more accurate climate models to predict weather patterns and changes.

Stating this, it is worth noting that quantum computing is not meant to replace classical computing but to complement it, solving problems that are currently out of reach for classical machines.

11.4. Predictive Landscape: Quantum Computing in the Future

If this era is dominated by classical computing, the next could very well be the age of quantum. It's reached a point where quantum computers, albeit in primitive form, are starting to show real promise. Google's 2019 announcement of quantum supremacy—being able to perform a specific task in 200 seconds, which would take the world's fastest supercomputer 10,000 years to complete—has already set a precedent in this field.

By the 2030s, it is highly plausible we will see a commercially viable quantum computer. While it's true that there are still significant barriers to overcome, the progress made already indicates a promising future for quantum computers. From here, we would expect to see more active participation from private and government sectors, deliberately funding and developing quantum technology and not as mere lab projects.

11.5. The Quantum Challenge: Crucial Considerations

Notwithstanding the potential of quantum computing, the path to establishing quantum technologies in everyday computing applications is plagued with challenges. These issues range from stability, where qubits need to operate under specific conditions (such as ultra-cold environments), to developing quantum algorithms and ensuring quantum error correction.

Moreover, robust security protocols need to be in place since quantum computers can crack most existing cryptographic systems. The fear of "quantum hacking" could lead to a version of the crypto wars we have seen with classical computers.

11.6. Perspectives: The Ongoing Debate

The potential of quantum computing is vast, but many scholars argue against overhyping its capabilities. Although it can solve certain problems faster, it is currently unclear how much of an advantage it would have over classical counterparts. Moreover, quantum computing is still in an embryonic stage, with multiple issues requiring attention: qubit stability, quantum-proof cryptography, robust quantum error correction techniques, etc.

However, despite these controversies, the possibilities quantum computing presents are undeniably enticing. Whether or not it eliminates traditional computing is immaterial. What is important is that it will tackle problems previously deemed impossible or too complex, thus opening up new capabilities.

In conclusion, whilst the journey towards the Quantum Age is fraught with complex challenges to overcome, one cannot deny the transformative power such a technology could have. The leaps in quantum computing technology witnessed today are on par with the evolution of classical computing half a century ago. As society, industry, and governments bet on quantum, we could well be witnessing the next great leap in the realm of technology. Only time will validate the anticipation surrounding this powerful technology.

Please note: As the quantum realm is continually evolving, it's recommended to keep updated with recent advances in this explosive field. [/note]

Quantum computing holds the potential to break barriers and catapult computation into an entirely new realm. Nonetheless, such potential only exists when met with earnest comprehension, deep study, and an understanding about the implications. This is your invitation to grasp the immense potential of the quantum future and explore the next great leap in computational science brought forth by quantum mechanics. Don't hesitate to jump into this fascinating world and join the wave of breakthroughs and innovation unveiled by this transformative technology.

www.ingramcontent.com/pod-product-compliance
Lightning Source LLC
Chambersburg PA
CBHW071010260726
48661CB00007B/2871